The North Yorkshire Moors Railway and The Esk Valley Line
Past and Present
Subscribers' Limited Edition

John Hunt

John Hunt

A PAST and PRESENT Companion

The NORTH YORKSHIRE MOORS RAILWAY & THE ESK VALLEY LINE

Past and Present

NORTH YORKSHIRE MOORS RAILWAY

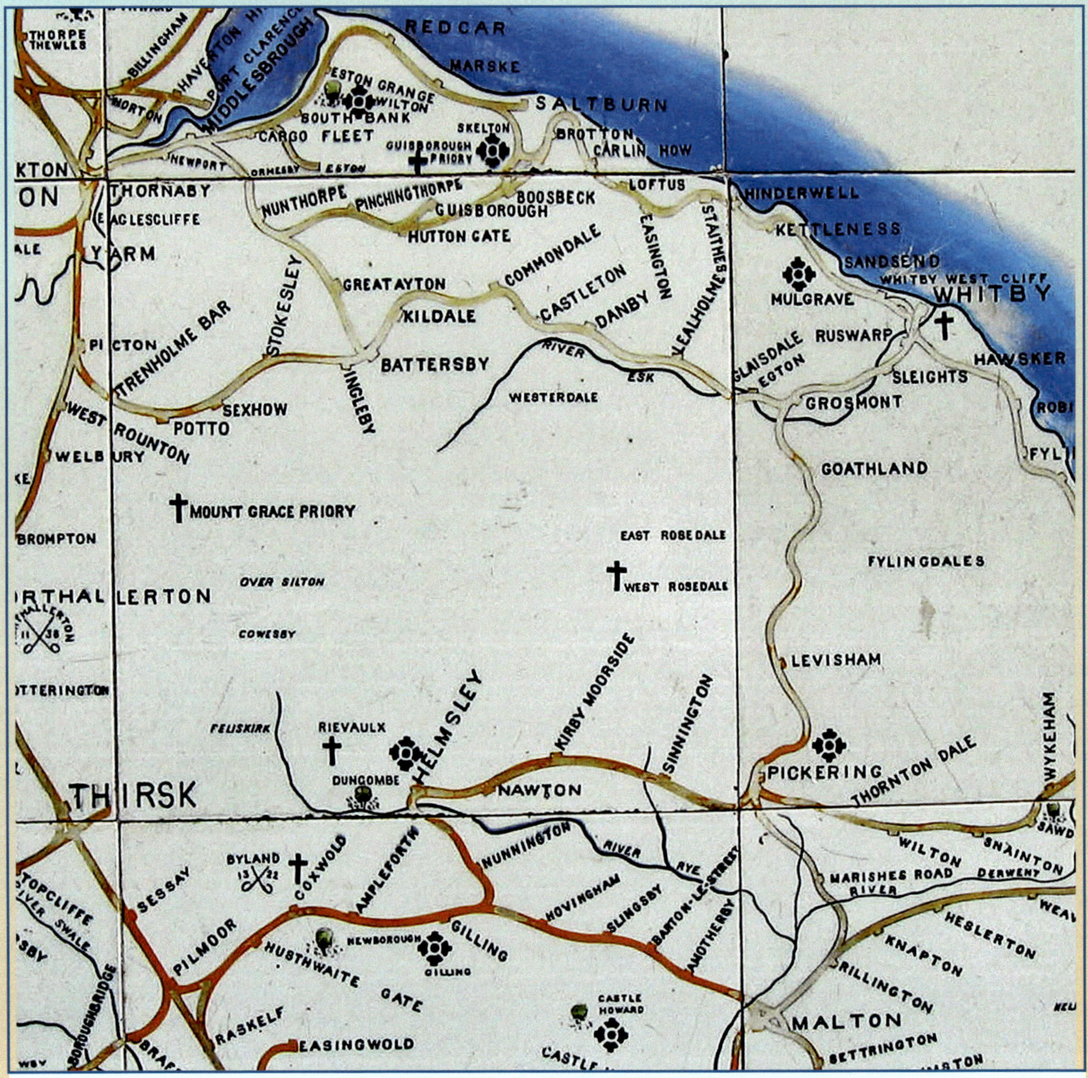

Above: This extract from the iconic NER tiled map shows how the lines from Whitby to Malton, Middlesbrough and Picton related to the NER network.

Half-title: A LNER tradition has been resurrected with the erection of a summit sign on the NYMR, similar to the iconic one at Stainmore Summit. Located close to the Lyke Wake Walk crossing at Fen Bog, the sign was lifted into place on 5 December 2016. Nick Carter and Bryan Blundell pose by the new sign. *Bryan Blundell*

A PAST and PRESENT Companion

The NORTH YORKSHIRE MOORS RAILWAY & THE ESK VALLEY LINE

Past and Present

John Hunt

Past & Present Publishing Ltd

© John Hunt 2017

All rights reserved. No part of this publication may be reproduced, stored in a retrieval system or transmitted, in any form or by any means, electronic, mechanical, photocopying, recording or otherwise, without prior permission in writing from Past & Present Publishing Ltd.

First published in 2017

British Library Cataloguing in Publication Data

A catalogue record for this book is available from the British Library.

ISBN 978 1 85895 299 4 (Softcover)
     978 1 85895 300 7 (Hardcover Limited Edition)

Past & Present Publishing Ltd
The Trundle
Ringstead Road
Great Addington
Kettering
Northants NN14 4BW

Tel/Fax: 01536 330588
email: ssilverlinkpublishing@btconnect.com
Website: www.nostalgiacollection.com

Printed and bound in the Czech Republic

Acknowledgements

In compiling this book the author is indebted to the following photographers: Michael Anderson, the late J. W. Armstrong, Philip Benham, the late John Boyes, Maurice Burns, Alan Brown, Nick Carter, P. Cookson, Frank Dean, C. M. Doncaster/NRM, the late Chris Gammell, David Idle, P. H. King, John Spencer Gilks, John F. Mallon, the late Michael Mensing, David Mitchell, Gavin Morrison, David Rodgers, Sidney Smith/Beck Isle Museum, Ken Snowdon, David Sutcliffe, Nigel Trotter, and for the Limited Edition the following: S. Barraclough, D. Birtle, B. Blundell, M. Braham, I. Broadhead, J. Colls, C. Donald, A. Frith, S. Kendall, T. Noble and J. Robertson.

In addition, the assistance of Richard Barber and John Midcalf of the JWA Trust is acknowledged.

'A1' No 60163 *Tornado* leaves Goathland on 5 May 2009. *John Hunt*

Contents

Introduction	6
Whitby to Grosmont	8
Grosmont to Goathland	19
Goathland to New Bridge, Pickering	36
Pickering to Malton	52
Grosmont to Battersby	66
Battersby to Picton	96
Battersby to Nunthorpe East Junction	121
Nunthorpe to Guisborough	131
Nunthorpe to Middlesbrough	140

A BBC filming special returning from Whitby to Leeds leaves Goathland on 13 April 1964, and East Midlands HST, headed by No 43044, passes through Goathland non stop on Saturday 15 July 2017 on a Derby - Pickering special: this was the very first occasion that a HST had traversed the Grosmont - Pickering line. *Gavin Morrison/Robin Patrick*

Introduction

Such is the wealth of photographic material that this is the fourth volume dedicated to the NYMR, and the second in colour. However, in a departure from the previous volumes the coverage not only looks at the Whitby to Malton line, including the past and present North Yorkshire Moors Railway, but has been widened to include the rest of the Esk Valley line from Grosmont, through to Battersby and Middlesbrough. En route there were two junctions, at Battersby and Nunthorpe East, so the respective lines to Picton and Guisborough are depicted as well.

Dr Beeching originally proposed that all railways serving Whitby should be closed, the coast line from Loftus having succumbed in 1958. In the event, the lines from Whitby to Scarborough and Grosmont to Rillington Junction did close, on 8 March 1965, but the Esk Valley line was reprieved. Preservationists eventually saw the Rillington line reopened from Grosmont to Pickering, as the North Yorkshire Moors Railway, and this history is précised in the opening chapter of this book.

While the economic and hardship case for closure of the lines from Whitby to Scarborough and Rillington was upheld, the reprieve for the line from Middlesbrough to Whitby was primarily based on the need to provide transport for schoolchildren from the villages in the Esk Valley to the secondary school in Whitby, a role it still performs today. However, the reprieve did not come without cost savings, and since 1965 the line from Nunthorpe has seen major rationalisation, with Whitby reduced from four platforms to just one, station staff withdrawn, the track singled between Whitby and Grosmont, the crossing loop at Castleton removed, and signalling and signal boxes replaced with the 'No Signaller Token System on Single Lines with Remote Crossing Loops' (NSTR), controlled from Nunthorpe signal box.

However, the fortunes of the 35-mile line have been turned round, since it is now supported by the Esk Valley Railway Development Company (EVRDC) set up in 2003, which was designated by the Department for Transport as a Community Rail Partnership in 2005. Apart from the essential service of bringing Esk Valley students to school, the number of visitors to Whitby has grown since 2003. The EVRDC promotes and markets the line, distributes timetables throughout the Esk Valley and highlights the need for an improved service. The opening of the new James Cook station has also emphasised the need for a better service and a year-round Sunday service to assist patients, visitors and hospital staff from the Esk Valley and Whitby to access James Cook University Hospital. The EVRDC is funded mainly by Northern Rail, as well as North Yorkshire County Council. Grants are awarded from time to time through the Association of Community Rail Partnerships (ACoRP), the Department for Transport and Network Rail.

Further EVRDC details are obtainable from: enquiries@eskvalleyrailway.co.uk.

K4 No 3442 *The Great Marquess* awaits departure from Whitby with the returning BBC filming special for Leeds on 13 April 1964 *John Boyes*

Introduction

Whitby, with B1 No 61276 heading the 18.54 to York on 14 May 1964, and the same viewpoint on 7 January 2014. Three of the tracks in the past picture remain, but the water tank, carriage sidings, Bog Hall signal box and signals have long gone, and much of the estuary of the River Esk has been reclaimed *John Spencer Gilks/ John Hunt*

Whitby to Grosmont

The line from Whitby to Malton was originally the Whitby & Pickering Railway of 26 May 1836. The line was connected to the rapidly developing national network when it was extended southwards to join the York-Scarborough line at Rillington Junction, opening on 1 July 1845. It had connections at Bog Hall, Whitby, with the lines to Loftus (opened 3 December 1883, closed 5 May 1958) and Scarborough (opened 16 July 1885, closed 8 March 1965); at Grosmont with the Esk Valley line to Middlesbrough (opened 2 October 1865); and at Mill Lane, Pickering, for the Forge Valley line to Seamer (opened 1 April 1882, closed 3 January 1950) and the line to Helmsley and Pilmoor (opened 1 April 1875, closed 31 January 1953).

In the meantime, the original rope-worked incline at Beckhole had proved a major stumbling block, so a 3½-mile Deviation line was built between Grosmont and Goathland, opening on 1 July 1865. The section of the original route between Grosmont and Beckhole, then Esk Valley, was retained for goods traffic until that also closed, on 18 September 1951.

The line flourished, with through coaches between London King's Cross and Whitby, and excursion traffic; there were even camping coaches for holidaymakers at Levisham, Goathland and Grosmont stations. However, following the war the rise in car ownership and burgeoning bus services meant a gradual decline in passenger traffic, which ultimately led to closure on 8 March 1965. However, local people, aggrieved that their protests had not staved off closure, set about trying to restore passenger services. The precursor was the now famous meeting in Tom Salmon's house in Ruswarp on 3 June 1967, followed by the public meeting held in Goathland village hall on 18 November that year, when the North Yorkshire Moors Railway Preservation Society was set up. The rest, they say, is history!

The Society quickly went from strength to strength: the first rolling stock – AC Cars railbus No W79978 – arrived on 9 August 1968, followed by the first steam engine – *Mirvale* – on 2 February 1969, traversing the whole line from Pickering to Grosmont in the process! That year volunteers were allowed access to the line, and over the next few years more locomotives and rolling stock arrived, and the track and stations were brought back into operation. A major step forward was on 1 May 1973, when the line was officially re-opened, and on 24 May 1975 steam trains once more travelled regularly between Grosmont and Pickering.

The next 30 years saw consolidation, with gradual and incremental improvements to rolling stock and infrastructure, and ever-increasing patronage, helped by worldwide exposure in TV series like *Heartbeat* and the first *Harry Potter* film. In 2007 another major milestone was the extension of NYMR sevices over Network Rail tracks to and from Whitby. In 2014 the clock was turned back, when a second platform was reinstated at Whitby station.

As the NYMR celebrates its 50 anniversary in 2017 it can reflect that it has come a long way since 1967; it now carries around 350,000 passengers each year, has an annual turnover of more than £5,000,000, employs more than 100 paid staff in the peak season, and is supported by an even greater number of volunteers, who actually run the trains, a far cry from the low point in its fortunes back in March 1965.

A more comprehensive history of the railway and further details about its services can be obtained from the NYMR website: www.nymr.co.uk.

The running-in board at Whitby station provided by the NYMR when the second platform was brought into use on 14 August 2014. *John Hunt*

In a busy scene in the summer of 1958, 'B1' No 61053 shunts empty stock into Platform 2, while two Metro-Cammell DMUs occupy Platforms 1 and 4.

In the 'present' view, dated 8 March 2015, No 76079 waits to depart from Platform 1 with the 11.50 service to Pickering, as 5MT No 45428 *Eric Treacy* arrives in Platform 2 with the 11.15 from Grosmont. The house on the skyline to the left of the signal post in the 'past' view is the same one seen above the first carriage in the 2015 view. *Michael Mensing/Philip Benham*

Two three-car Metro-Cammell DMUs await departure from Whitby's Platform 3 on 8 August 1966, while in the 'present' view Class 66 No 66168 stands in the station with a Network Rail test train in June 2005. The house on the skyline on the extreme left and St Mary's church to the left of the signal box are common to both pictures. *Frank Dean/John Hunt*

Whitby to Grosmont

'B1' No 61275 enters Platform 2 at Whitby with the 4.00pm train from Malton some time in 1964. In the 'present' view, 'K1' No 62005 arrives with a train from Pickering on 28 April 2014. The houses on the skyline to the left of the signal box are the same as those above the coaches in the more recent picture. A Co-op store now occupies the former Platforms 3 and 4. *John Boyes/John Hunt*

BR Standard 2-6-0 No 77004 waits to leave Whitby at Bog Hall with the pick-up goods on 8 August 1963, and a year later two three-car Metro-Cammell DMUs pass Bog Hall crossing with a service to Middlesbrough. *Alan Brown/John Spencer Gilks*

Whitby to Grosmont

On 14 May 1964 'B1' No 61276 awaits its next duty as a DMU departs forming the 4.26pm Scarborough-Middlesbrough service. On 2 August 1981, passing the same signal, 'Deltic' No 55002 *The King's Own Yorkshire Light Infantry* leaves Whitby with a 'Merrymaker' excursion returning to Newcastle. Following arrival from Newcastle, it had earlier done a Whitby-Middlesbrough return trip. *John Boyes/John Hunt*

A Whitby & Pickering Railway weigh-house stood between the railway and the River Esk at Larpool, and is seen here in the early part of the twentieth century. The sad remains of the building are pictured on 13 March 2014. *Frank Dean collection/John Hunt*

Whitby to Grosmont

A DMU hugs the banks of the River Esk at Larpool in August 1964, forming a Whitby-Middlesbrough service, while on 7 March 2015 'K4' No 61994 *The Great Marquess* comes under Larpool Viaduct with a special train to mark the 50th anniversary of the closure of the Pickering line. *Frank Dean/Michael Anderson*

Seen looking westwards from the top of Larpool Viaduct, 'K1' No 2005 brings an excursion from London St Pancras towards Whitby, which it had worked from Battersby, on 28 June 1975.

Forty years later BR No 76079, with No D7628 on the rear, works a Santa special alongside the River Esk on 13 December 2015. *Chris Gammell/Ken Snowdon*

Two three-car Metro Cammell DMUs cross the River Esk at Ruswarp with a Middlesbrough-Whitby service on 9 August 1966.

In the second view two Class 142 DMUs approach Ruswarp with a Middlesbrough-Whitby service in the 1980s.

Finally, No D6515 crosses the Esk with the 09.10 Grosmont-Whitby train on 19 September 2011.
Frank Dean/ John Hunt/ Ken Snowdon/

The first view shows Sleights station as seen from the A169 Pickering-Whitby road bridge, looking east, on 4 May 1966, and the coal yard looks well stocked.

In the 'present' view, taken on 30 April 2016, BR No 76084 accelerates away with a Whitby-Pickering service. Tree growth has proliferated and has hidden the now disused coal yard, and though the tracks have been lifted the down platform and signal box still stand. *Frank Dean/Dave Rodgers*

Grosmont to Goathland

The engine crews of the Royal reopening train of 1 May 1973 headed by 'P3' No 2392 and ex-NCB No 29 engage in conversation as they await departure, viewed from Platform 1 at Grosmont, with the signal box on the right. *John Spencer Gilks*

In this view inside Grosmont signal box in 1964, the diagram clearly shows the junction of single-track Esk Valley line with the double track to Levisham. *John Spencer Gilks*

In May 1976 the Class 47 diesel hauling this PW train became derailed just after passing through Grosmont station en route to Glaisdale. Ex-NCB No 29 came to the rescue by removing the wagons to allow rerailing to begin.

On 5 February 2014 Class 66 No 66001 passes through Platform 1 at Grosmont with a train of ballast from Tees Yard to an NYMR track relaying site at Levisham. *Both John Hunt*

Grosmont to Goathland

A Northern Rail Class 143 DMU leaves Grosmont for Whitby as BR No 75029 runs round its NYMR train on 11 April 2002. In the second, more recent picture LNER 'A4' No 60019 *Bittern* awaits its next duty as 'Q6' No 63395 runs round its train having arrived from Pickering in April 2008. *Both John Hunt*

LMS 2-6-4T No 42085 waits for the signal with the 10.28am York-Whitby train on 1 August 1958.
On 16 May 1993 Class 31 Nos 31413 and 31417 lead an excursion from Whitby to the Settle & Carlisle line into Grosmont. *Michael Mensing/John Hunt*

Grosmont to Goathland

Two NYMR milestone events: in the first picture *Mirvale* pulls a Hull & Barnsley Railway coach through the station on 2 February 1969, the historic day it travelled through from Pickering. Not only was it the first steam engine over the line since closure, but also formed the first 'passenger' train!

In the second view 'P3' No 2392 pilots ex-NCB No 29 into the station with the Royal reopening train on 1 May 1973. The Duchess of Kent joined the train via the flower-bedecked ramp in the foreground. In the background stands the AC Cars railbus No W79978, which had been the first preserved vehicle to arrive, on 9 August 1968. *Both John Hunt*

The first three steam locomotives to arrive on the NYMR are pictured in the platforms at Grosmont in March 1969; from the left, they are Borrows well tank No 3, Andrew Barclay 0-6-0 *Salmon* and Hudswell Clark 0-4-0 *Mirvale*.

On 25 October 1971 'P3' No 2392 (right) is viewed from the signal protecting the level crossing during the handing over ceremony. Note 'Q6' No 3395, ex-NCB Nos 29 and 5 in Platform 2, and the washing across the run-round loop on the right! *John Boyes/John Hunt*

Grosmont to Goathland

An unidentified 'B1' 4-6-0 leaves Grosmont for Pickering, Malton and York in 1963. The second pictures shows the scene on the morning of 2 February 1969 pending the historic arrival of *Mirvale* later that day. *John Spencer Gilks/John Hunt*

On 21 March 1970 *Salmon* heads wagons from the Whitby pick-up goods conveying the dismantled shearlegs from Tweedmouth MPD, purchased by the North Eastern Locomotive Preservation Group (NELPG) and about to be unloaded for re-erection at Grosmont. On the right is Deviation signal box.

Seen from the same vantage point on 7 November 2013, the white-painted houses on the left horizon are common to both pictures. Tunnel Cottages and Deviation signal box have gone, replaced by the MPD buildings comprising the repair and running sheds to the left, and the wheel drop, coaling plant and NELPG's Deviation shed to the right. In the foreground is the Armstrong Oilers building. *Maurice Burns/John Hunt*

Grosmont to Goathland

Former NCB No 31 *Meteor*, with some assistance from No D5032 at the rear, works hard up the 1 in 49 gradient at Beckhole in April 1977, while visiting 'A3' No 60103 *Flying Scotsman* rounds the same curve on 17 March 2016. *Both John Hunt*

In the summer of 1964 a 'B1' 4-6-0 heads the 2.12pm Whitby-Leeds train at Water Ark, while in the summer of 1976 'J52' No 1247 drifts down the 1 in 49 with the BR weedkilling train returning from Pickering. *David Sutcliffe/John Hunt*

Grosmont to Goathland

This is Darnholm road bridge looking north in the winter of 1967, two years after closure. In the second view LNER 'Pacific' No 60532 *Blue Peter* passes the same spot in November 2001. *Frank Dean/John Hunt*

A DMU forming the 12.01 service to Malton awaits departure from Goathland on 5 March 1965. Half a century later, on 17 February 2015, a preserved Metro-Cammell DMU stands in the same place with a Grosmont-Pickering service. Note the addition of the footbridge in the preservation era and the perpetuation of the LNER and BR tradition of locating a camping coach here. *Frank Dean/John Hunt*

Grosmont to Goathland

Fifty years of change at Goathland. In the first view a Class 24 passes through in the late summer of 1964 with a train from Leeds to Whitby, while in the second the AC Cars railbus stands in the platform in 1971.

On 19 February 2015 a three-car Metro-Cammell DMU awaits departure for Grosmont. *David Sutcliffe/ P. H. King/John Hunt*

Photographed from the bracket signal seen in the second picture, AC Cars railbus No W79978, still in BR livery, is prepared for an historic run to Pickering with the 'Phoenix' special on 20 July 1969.

In the early days of the infant NYMR, before a motive power depot was established at Grosmont, the up sidings at Goathland were used to stable, prepare and dispose of the steam locomotives. Here, ex-NCB No 5 backs down onto its carriages as 'Q6' No 3395 and No 3 raise steam in the summer of 1971. *John Boyes/David Idle*

Grosmont to Goathland

A three-car DMU forming the 12.01 service to Malton leaves a snowy Goathland on 5 March 1965. Almost exactly 50 years later, on 17 February 2015, the NYMR's Metro-Cammell DMU departs with a Grosmont-Pickering service. *Frank Dean/John Hunt*

Ex-NCB No 29 shunts the depot siding at Goathland in April 1992, while on 5 February 2014 Class 66 No 66001 passes through 'wrong line' with a train of ballast from Tees Yard to a track relaying site at Levisham. *Both John Hunt*

Grosmont to Goathland

GNR 'J52' No 1247 arrives at Goathland with a train from Pickering in September 1976. Since then, the coniferous trees have been felled and the signal replaced with a fine three-way NER bracket signal, as a visiting Class 220 'Virgin Voyager' enters the station from Pickering in May 2002. *Both John Hunt*

Goathland to New Bridge, Pickering

Two-car Gloucester and three-car Metro-Cammell DMUs pass Moorgates forming a Grosmont-Pickering service in the winter of 1973, and at the same location No D7628 heads an empty ballast train, with No 66078 on the rear, from Levisham back to Grosmont on 8 March 2017. *NYMR/John Hunt*

Goathland to New Bridge, Pickering

'Q6' No 3395 heads a short train at Eller Beck in August 1971, then 'B1' No 61264 is seen at the head of a mixed train at the same location on 15 November 2013. *Both John Hunt*

Two two-car DMUs, with a six-wheeled van at the rear, emerge from Northdale and make their way towards Whitby at Fen Bog, the summit of the line, in the summer of 1964.

In the foreground is the Lyke Wake Walk, being passed by an unidentified 'B1' in August 1964 with a train from Whitby to Malton or York.

From a slightly higher viewpoint along the path, 'K1' No 62005 heads the LNER teak coaches towards Grosmont on 26 March 2008. *Frank Dean (2)/John Hunt*

Goathland to New Bridge, Pickering

Looking northwards at milepost 18 at the top of Northdale in the summer of 1964, on the right can be seen the reed beds that signify the approach to Fen Bog. A similar view was obtained from the AC Cars railbus in July 1971 after the old down line had been removed; the same milepost can just be discerned. *Frank Dean/John Hunt*

A three-car Metro-Cammell DMU passes through Northdale on 26 May 1973 forming a service from Pickering High Mill to Grosmont. At this time there was no access to Pickering station, so trains used a temporary platform at High Mill. DMUs had to be used as there was no run round loop or engine release road at High Mill.

In the second picture Class 14 No D9523 heads southbound into Northdale with a Grosmont-Pickering train in August 1983. Looking at the dry grass and almost cloudless sky, the diesel was probably being used due to a high fire risk.

Finally we see 'J72' No 69023 banking a Grosmont-bound afternoon train out of Northdale in the autumn of 1987. *David Idle/John Hunt (2)*

Newton Dale signal box is seen first in 1964, then in 1970 as AC Cars railbus No W79978 passes the now increasingly derelict building. *Frank Dean/John Boyes*

The original NER signal box diagram. *John Boyes*

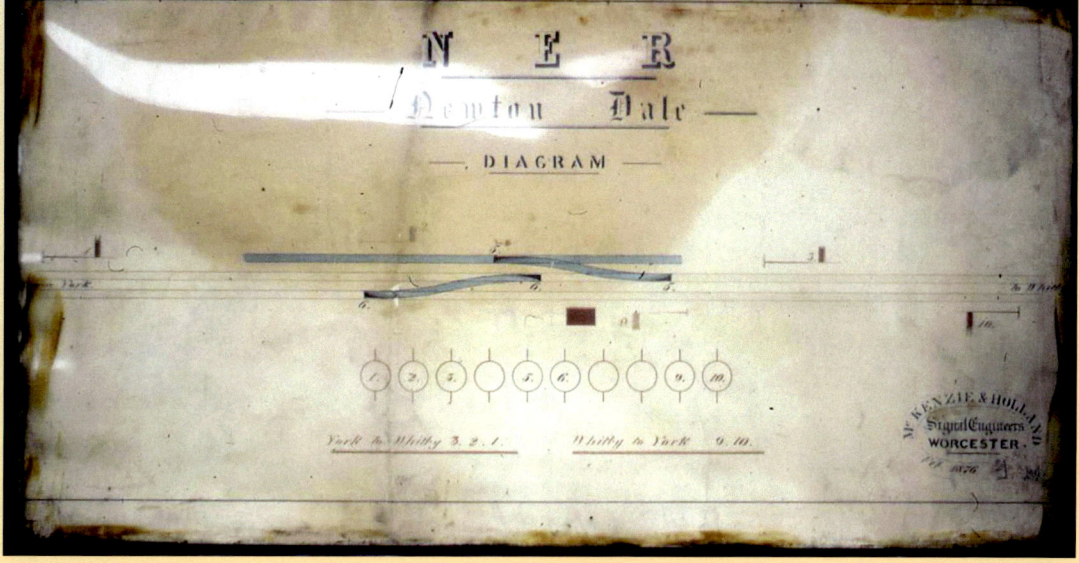

An unidentified 'B1' heads north through Newtondale with the London King's Cross-Malton-Whitby train in the summer of 1963. From the same viewpoint on 22 May 1977 we see the 'Q6', as 'T2' No 2238, heading south towards Levisham. *David Sutcliffe/John Hunt*

Goathland to New Bridge, Pickering

The view from a northbound DMU near milepost 14 in the heart of Newtondale dates from the winter of 1963. In very different weather at the same location in 1970 we see an early NYMR inspection of the line by railbus. *David Sutcliffe/John Boyes*

The Grange, a mile north of Levisham, is pictured after closure, on 10 June 1967, whilst the corresponding 'present' view shows track relaying using steel sleepers on 15 November 2016. *Frank Dean/Nigel Trotter*

After the lifting of the second track in 1969 is was necessary to relay track and provide turnouts to create a passing loop at Levisham. Here the down line is extended by volunteers early in 1974, and on 23 February of that year ex-NCB No 5 brings a works train over the newly installed pointwork. *Both John Hunt*

A York to Whitby DMU stands at Levisham in April 1964, while the scene in June 1989 shows GWR No 6619 (left) awaiting the arrival of SR No 841 from Grosmont before proceeding north. Note the signalman exchanging the single-line tokens. *John Spencer Gilks/John Hunt*

Goathland to New Bridge, Pickering

'D49' 4-4-0 No 255 *Braes of Derwent* heads a southbound train at Levisham station in the 1920s; note the camping coach on the right. In a similar view, a DMU forms the 12.16 service to Malton on 2 March 1965. *Frank Dean collection/Frank Dean*

A desolate but tidy scene at Levisham is captured in 1964, then ten years later in 1974 the up starting signal, siding and headshunt have gone, but Gloucester and Metro-Cammell DMUs pass the same spot. *David Mitchell/John Hunt*

Goathland to New Bridge, Pickering

'K4' No 3442 *The Great Marquess* has stopped for examination and photographs at Farwath on 13 April 1964 with the BBC filming train from Leeds to Whitby and back.
 On 31 December 2016 'Q6' No 63395 passes the same spot with a Pickering-Grosmont train. *Gavin Morrison/John Hunt*

This is New Bridge signal box, Pickering, looking north, with the signalman's transport parked outside on 29 May 1965. In the second picture the box and crossing are seen from the front of a DMU on 2 March of the same year. *Both Frank Dean*

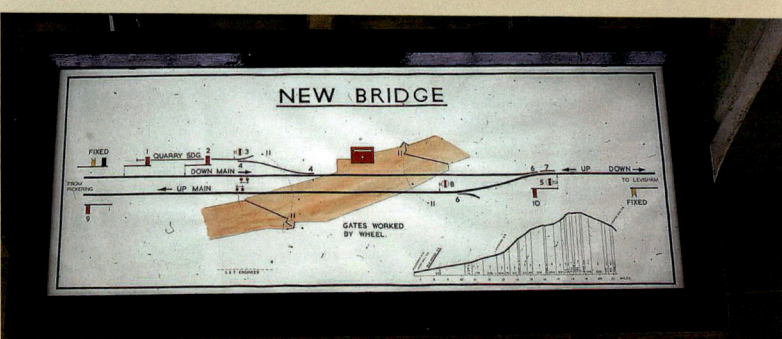

The signalling diagram inside New Bridge signal box, showing the double track from Pickering reducing to single track towards Levisham, the siding into New Bridge quarry, and the gradient profile. *John Boyes*

Goathland to New Bridge, Pickering

Ex-NCB No 5 brings an empty stock train over New Bridge crossing on 23 February 1974, while in the second view BR No 75029 rolls past the signal box with a train from Grosmont to Pickering in January 2001, using the former up line. The old down line used by No 5 is now a siding from New Bridge yard and ends the far side of the level crossing. *Both John Hunt*

Pickering to Malton

In the first of these three photographs 'V2' No 60886 runs round the Royal Train in Pickering station on 3 July 1965, and in the second, 'P3' No 2392 does likewise with the Royal NYMR re-opening train on 1 May 1973. Finally, ex-LMS 5MT 4-6-0 No 5428 *Eric Treacy* draws the BR weedkilling train into the station on 6 May 1974. *Frank Dean/ John Hunt (2)*

On 1 October 1963 'B1' No 61021 *Reitbok* arrives with an RCTS/SLS 'North Eastern' tour.

Just under two years later, on 3 July 1965, four months after closure to passengers, 'V2' No 60886 is seen again pulling the empty stock of the Royal Train into the station. It had been used by the Duke of Edinburgh.

In the third view ex-NCB No 5 stands in the station on 23 July 1971 after working through from Grosmont with a train carrying local politicians canvassing support for the fledgling NYMR. *David Mitchell/Frank Dean/John Hunt*

NORTH YORKSHIRE MOORS RAILWAY

'B1' No 61049 enters Pickering station with a train from Whitby to York on 13 April 1964. Fifty years later, the platforms have been extended northwards over the Pickering Beck, but seen from a similar vantage point 5MT No 45428 *Eric Treacy* arrives with a train from Whitby on 29 October 2014. *David Mitchell/John Hunt*

Pickering to Malton

In the first picture, Pickering station looks neat and tidy, belying the fact that this is the penultimate day of passenger operation, 5 March 1965.

On 16 October 2014 GWR 'Castle' Class No 5029 *Nunney Castle* has arrived beneath the G. T. Andrews-style overall roof rebuilt in 2010/11. *Frank Dean/John Hunt*

Pickering station is viewed from the cab of No D2066 working the last train to New Bridge quarry on 1 July 1966.

Seven years later 'P3' No 2392 and ex-NCB No 29 have arrived with the Royal re-opening train from Grosmont on 1 May 1973. In the other platform stands BR Standard 2-6-4T No 80135, which had been purchased from Barry scrapyard the previous year. *Frank Dean/John Hunt*

Pickering to Malton

These views of the station are looking north from Bridge Street, first in October 1964, then from a similar vantage point in January 2010, with No D7628 blanketed in snow and a stores van where the loading dock used to be. *Frank Dean/John Hunt*

Pickering scenes: *Top right:* No D2066 propels its train past High Mill en route to New Bridge quarry for the final time on 1 July 1966; *Middle right:* the inside of Bridge Street signal box; *Top middle:* the goods yard crane; *Top left:* the combined signal and telegraph pole opposite the goods shed; *Above:* Hungate signal box; *Left:* Bridge Street signal box (with the Royal Train stabled beyond it); and *Middle right:* High Mill signal box. *All Frank Dean*

Pickering to Malton

These are both 'past' scenes, there being no 'present' viewpoint, but they are included for completeness to illustrate the railway scene in Pickering. The first shows the single-road engine shed, which still stands today, while in the second No D2066 collects wagons from the coal drops; both pictures were taken on 1 July 1966, the final day that the goods train was to run. In the background can be seen Hungate level crossing and the goods shed. *Both Frank Dean*

Marishes Road was the only intermediate station between Pickering and Rillington. In the first view a Metro-Cammell DMU from Whitby arrives in January 1965.

    The second picture captures the end of an era – the guard closes the gates for the last time as No D2066 works the final pick-up goods back to Malton on 1 July 1966. *Both Frank Dean*

Pickering to Malton

Scenes at Marishes Road in January 1965: *Clockwise from above:* the immaculate lever frame; an old enamel sign; the signal protecting the siding; the signal box diagram; and a general view of the station. *All Frank Dean*

The goods siding on the up side of Marishes Road station was still in use in January 1965, but closed from 8 March that year.

The same view on 17 December 2013 shows that the concrete gate post, on the right of both pictures, still stands. *Frank Dean/John Hunt*

Pickering to Malton

The line from Whitby joined the York-Scarborough line at Rillington Junction. The junction and station are seen from the 08.55 Whitby-Malton train headed by English Electric Type 4 (later Class 40) No D259 on 6 March 1965, the last day of passenger services between Grosmont and Malton.

In the more recent picture GWR 'Hall' Class No 5972 *Olton Hall* passes the same spot with an afternoon 'Scarborough Spa Express' from York on 21 August 2002. *Maurice Burns/John Hunt*

Looking west, two three-car Metro-Cammell DMUs call at Malton station in 1966 with a service for Scarborough. At that time the station still had its overall roof and island platform.

On 19 December 2013 a TransPennine Class 185 calls with a Scarborough-Liverpool service. In the intervening period the island platform and overall roof have gone, part of the platform has been raised and some of the windows boarded up. *John Spencer Gilks/John Hunt*

Pickering to Malton

On 26 August 1958 4MT 2-6-0 No 43077 heads east out of Malton station with a goods train bound for Scarborough.

In the second view No 3440 *City of Truro* leaves Malton after a 20-minute stop with the afternoon Malton Dickens Christmas Festival special from York to Scarborough on 20 December 1986.

Finally, Class 158 No 158812 departs from Malton with a TransPennine service to Scarborough in March 2001. *P. Cookson/John Hunt (2)*

Grosmont to Battersby

The 17¾-mile line from Grosmont to Battersby consists of the Grosmont & Castleton branch, opened by the NER on 2 October 1865, which met the North Yorkshire & Cleveland Railway at Castleton, thus providing a through route between Whitby and the Leeds Northern main line at Picton. The final section of the NY&CR had opened to Castleton in 1861, two years after the NER had taken it over.

From Grosmont the line regularly swaps sides with the River Esk until it reaches Glaisdale, the only remaining crossing loop. Just beyond, in a field on the north side, a stone overbridge marks the aborted Cleveland Extension Mineral Railway from Lingdale, also known as 'Paddy Waddell's Railway' after its contractor. Started in the 1870s, construction ceased when only a few earthworks had been completed.

The line then passes through stations at Lealholm and Danby, before reaching Castleton Moor, where there was another passing loop until 1982. At the next station, Commondale, a short branch crossed the river and went northwards to a brickworks. After Commondale the line traverses Kildale Moor and the summit of the line at 582 feet above sea level; then, just under 2 miles after Kildale, the line joins the single line from Nunthorpe and runs into Battersby. Until 1965 the line continued on to Stokesley.

From Battersby, a 14-mile line ran to Rosedale. It opened in 1861 and from Ingleby Greenhow it ascended a rope-worked incline, 1 in 5 at its steepest, to the moors, where it continued at well over 1,000 feet above sea level to the mines and calcining kilns at West and East Rosedale.

A general view of Grosmont in 1964: the line to Pickering goes towards the bottom of the picture, disappearing into the tunnel beneath the near field. The Esk valley line diverges to the left adjacent to the signal box. The tree-covered area above the houses to the left of the station was the site of Grosmont iron works. *David Sutcliffe*

Grosmont to Battersby

The first station west of Grosmont is Egton, and in the first picture a motley-liveried DMU forming a Middlesbrough-Whitby service calls to pick up passengers some time in the winter of 1973.

On 24 February 2016 Class 66 No 66152 passes through with a ballast train for the NYMR. *John Spencer Gilks/John Hunt*

Just east of Glaisdale the railway runs through the gorge of the River Esk, and in doing so crosses the river three times. The middle of the three bridges – No 82 – is seen here with 'G5' 0-4-4T No 67343 crossing with a Stockton-Whitby train in August 1953.

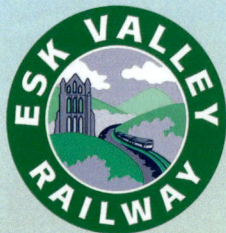

The bridge is viewed again from the cab of 'K1' No 62005 on 15 March 2015. The original stone-built bridge was washed away on 23 July 1930 and replaced by a single-span girder bridge. Severe flooding a year later on 5 September 1931 washed away the supporting pier and the steel span fell, undamaged, into the river bed. It was rebuilt using the undamaged section, but with an additional girder span, and the bridge survives today. *J. W. Armstrong/John Hunt*

This is Glaisdale station, looking west, in April 1974 and on 24 February 2016. On 13 April 1986 all the signals were taken out of use and hydraulic run-through points were installed. Remarkably, other than the removal of the semaphore signals, replacement of the lamps and provision of the ubiquitous shelter, little has changed in the intervening years. Nowadays Glaisdale is the only remaining passing place between Battersby and Whitby. *John Spencer Gilks/John Hunt*

In the first of these three views 'K1' No 2005 stands at Glaisdale on 29 March 1982 with a Gloucester DMU and No D5032, returning from tyre-turning at Thornaby, and 'P3' No 2392, which the 'K1' had hauled from York.

On 22 December 2009 No D7628 waits to cross the midday service from Whitby with a Santa Special; 'Schools' Class No 30926 *Repton* was on the rear of the train.

Finally, Class 66 No 66152, with a ballast train for the NYMR, waits to cross the 08.45 off Whitby on 24 February 2016. *All John Hunt*

Looking east at Glaisdale in August 1953 'G5' 0-4-4T No 67262 has arrived with a late-morning service from Whitby, while in the second picture B1 No 61264 stands in exactly the same place with a NYMR crew training special on 4th February 2017. Whilst the name board has gone, the signal box and waiting shelter on the down platform remain. *J.W. Armstrong/ John Hunt*

With the village cricket team in action, 'K1' No 2005 leaves Glaisdale with a return Whitby-London St Pancras tour on 28 June 1975; it worked the train as far as Battersby.

Seen from the same viewpoint, Class 156 No 156443 forms the 12.18 Whitby-Middlesbrough service on 24 February 2016. *Chris Gammell/John Hunt*

Grosmont to Battersby

'Schools' Class 4-4-0 No 30926 *Repton* heads north out of Glaisdale with a Whitby-Battersby special on 21 March 2010. The water on the left lies in a shallow cutting that comprised the earthworks for what became known as 'Paddy Waddell's Railway'.

In the second picture, taken from the far end of the water shown in the top picture, the hedge beside the Esk Valley line is on the left, and it can be seen that another overbridge was constructed, togther with further earthworks on either side of the River Esk, before the scheme was aborted. Started in the 1870s, the ill-fated Cleveland Extension Mineral Railway was originally intended to connect Glaisdale with Lingdale. *Ken Snowdon/ John Hunt*

A pair of 142 DMUs cross the River Esk between Lealholm and Glaisdale with a Middlesbrough – Whitby train in the summer of 1997.

At the same location on 11 January 2017 Class 156 No 156479 forms the 12.15 Whitby-Middlesbrough service. *Both John Hunt*

Two Metro-Cammell DMUs approach Lealholm forming a Whitby-Middlesbrough service in April 1980, then 36 years later Class 156 DMU No 156490 passes the same spot with the 12.15 service from Whitby to Middlesbrough (despite the destination blind) on 1 December 2016. *John Spencer Gilks/John Hunt*

A three-car Metro-Cammell DMU leaves Lealholm forming a service to Whitby Town in April 1968, then on 1 December 2016 Class 156 No 156490 is seen again departing as the 10.28 Middlesbrough-Whitby service. In the intervening years tree growth has all but hidden the railway house on the left, but the station remains little changed. *John Spencer Gilks/John Hunt*

Grosmont to Battersby

A Gloucester DMU calls at Lealholm in May 1976 for passengers to inspect and photograph the train and the station. The latter is little altered as 'Schools' Class No 30926 *Repton* speeds through on 7 March 2010 with a Whitby-Battersby special. Note the evidence of the second platform and passing loop. *John Spencer Gilks/Ken Snowdon*

'P3' No 2392 pilots No D6874 on the Whitby-Tees Yard pick-up goods near Lealholm on 29 August 1972; the 'P3' had been put on the train at Grosmont and was going to the Open Day at Thornaby motive power depot held on 10 September of that year.

On 28 February 2016 No D7628 heads a Grosmont-Whitby-Battersby NYMR crew-training special. *John Spencer Gilks/John Hunt*

Grosmont to Battersby

NYMR-bound, with a little assistance from 'Q6' No 63395, Class 37 No D6899 and ex-NCB No 29 make leisurely progress at Houlsyke between Danby and Lealholm on 25 June 1970, as the cattle take notice.

In exactly the same place, 47 years later, D7628 leads two coaches and 'B1' No 61264 back from Battersby to Grosmont on a NYMR crew training run on 4 February 2017. It is not just the location which is common to both pictures, since the young BR fireman on 29 was Chris Cubitt, who was also the driver on D7628 nearly half a century later! *Both John Hunt*

Just east of Danby the line crosses the River Esk again. In the first picture a three-car Class 144 DMU heads eastwards in December 1998; in the middle picture Class 66 No 66152 brings up the rear of empty ballast hoppers returning to Tees Yard from the NYMR on 24 February 2016; and finally a Class 156 DMU forms the 14.04 Middlesbrough-Whitby service on 5 January 2017. Seen above the bridge is the National Park Centre.

The bridge is one of no fewer than nine that cross the Esk between Grosmont and Castleton. This example, together with three similar single spans (identical to the NYMR's bridge No 30) – Duck at Danby, and Thorneywaite and Carr End at Glaisdale – were replaced in June 2012. *John Spencer Gilks/John Hunt (2)*

Grosmont to Battersby

A mixed-liveried Metro-Cammell DMU approaches Danby station as a service from Whitby to Middlesbrough in April 1968. At the same location, heavily disguised by more than 40 years of tree growth, Class 156 No 156490 forms the 12.15 Whitby-Middlesbrough service on 29 November 2016. *John Spencer Gilks/John Hunt*

In April 1968 a Metro-Cammell DMU calls at Danby station with a Middlesbrough-Whitby service, then 10 years later in September 1978 two 'Pacer' DMUs arrive forming a Whitby service. On 29 November 2016 Class 156 No 156490 is seen providing the 10.28 service from Middlesbrough to Whitby. In the intervening years the monkey puzzle tree has grown appreciably, but the signal box and lineside huts have gone. *John Spencer Gilks (2)/John Hunt*

Grosmont to Battersby

East of Castleton, Class 47 No 47474 heads towards Whitby with a return excursion from Edinburgh on 17 July 1993.

In the second picture Class 66 No 66157 is conveying the new beams for the NYMR's bridge 30 between Grosmont and Goathland, together with a heavyweight Kirow crane, on 4 January 2010.

Finally, Class 156 No 156490 heads east in somewhat better weather conditions forming the 10.28 Middlesbrough-Whitby service on 23 January 2017. *John Spencer Gilks/John Hunt (2)*

On 29 March 1982 'K1' No 2005 brings a Gloucester DMU, Class 24 No D5032 and 'P3' No 2392 into Castleton station.
From a similar vantage point Class 156 No 156443 is seen arriving with the 10.28 Middlesbrough-Whitby service on 24 February 2016. *Both John Hunt*

Grosmont to Battersby

EE Type 3 (later Class 37) No D6778 stands at Castleton during a photo stop on 6 May 1967, hauling the RCTS 'North Eastern No 3 Railtour' returning to Bradford from Whitby; the diesel had taken over from 'Jubilee' No 45562 *Alberta* at Middlesbrough and worked the train to Skinningrove and Whitby before returning to Middlesbrough.

Seen from the same vantage point on 12 January 2017, Class 156 No 156484 forms the 12.15 Whitby-Middlesbrough service. The crossing loop, siding, signals and signal box were removed in July 1982. *John Spencer Gilks/John Hunt*

Pictured approaching Commondale from Castleton is 'K1' No 2005 with a Whitby-Battersby special train on 8 June 1975. In the corresponding 'present' picture Class 156 No 156490 passes forming the 12.15 Whitby-Middlesbrough service on 1 December 2016. Note in the bottom right-hand corner the change from the white-painted LNER milepost 18 (from Picton) to the modern Network Rail yellow version. *Both John Hunt*

Grosmont to Battersby

In April 1973 ex-NCB No 29, 'Q6' No 3395 and 'P3' No 2392 make their way across Kildale Moor en route from Grosmont to Newcastle, where they were exhibited in Central station as part of the Newcastle Festival.

Two years later, on 28 June 1975, 'K1' No 2005 brings the returning Whitby-London St Pancras excursion through Kildale Moor; the 'K1' worked the train as far as Battersby.

In the third more recent view 'B1' No 61264 heads the 'Esk Valley Explorer' rail tour towards Kildale on 22 March 2014; on the rear of the train is 'K4' No 61994 *The Great Marquess*. All John Hunt

In the first of these three panoramic views Type 3 (later Class 37) No D6899 leads ex-NCB No 29 and 'Q6' No 63395 downhill across Kildale Moor towards Commondale on 25 June 1970.

On 22 March 2014 'K4' No 61994 *The Great Marquess* has just come over the summit en route to Whitby with the 'Esk Valley Explorer' rail tour; as seen in the previous pictures, 'B1' No 61264 was on the other end of the train.

In the third picture Class 25 No D7628 is seen retuning from Battersby to Grosmont with an NYMR crew-training run on 28 February 2016. *All John Hunt*

In February 1993 Class 31 No 31439 approaches Guisborough Road crossing, between Commondale and Kildale, with an excursion from Whitby, then a few years later on 12 December 1997 'Hastings' diesel-electric multiple unit No 1001 is seen at the same place with a special working from Middlesbrough. *to Whitby*

Twenty years later, on 5 January 2017, Class 156 No 156451 passes forming the 12.15 Whitby-Middlesbrough service. *John Spencer Gilks/John Hunt (2)*

Looking towards Guisborough Road crossing, seen in the distance, between Kildale and Commondale, Class 31 No 31240 heads a rather lightly loaded pick-up goods from Tees Yard to Whitby in April 1983.

In the second view Type 3 (later Class 37) No D6700 hauls GWR inspection saloon No 80974, 'J52' No 1247 and 'Black Five' No 5428 to the NYMR at Grosmont on 5 November 1973. The consist had originated at Tyseley, Birmingham, behind No D1818, with D6700 taking over at York.

The third picture is another view of 'K1' No 2005 hauling the Gloucester two-car DMU, Class 24 No D5032 and 'P3' No 2392 towards Grosmont on 29 March 1982.

Finally, Class 156 No 156451 forms the 10.28 Middlesbrough-Whitby service on 5 January 2017. *John Spencer Gilks/John Hunt (3)*

'A8' 4-6-2T No 69861 arrives at Kildale station in the early 1950s with a Middlesbrough-Whitby, then more than 60 years later Class 156 DMU No 156490 calls with the 10.28 Middlesbrough-Whitby service on 23 January 2017. Note that the supports for the station nameboard still stand. *J.W. Armstrong/John Hunt*

The same trains that featured in the previous pictures are seen again in the station. Note the substantial station buildings, signal box and goods yard off to the right – all were removed following the reduction of the station to an unstaffed halt in 1956. In the present-day view just a single platform and simple shelter suffice for passengers. *J. W. Armstrong/John Hunt*

Grosmont to Battersby

A Metro-Cammell DMU accelerates away from Kildale with a Whitby-Middlesbrough service. The bridge in the background is the one depicted on page 95.

In the second picture 'K1' No 2005 passes with the return excursion from Whitby to London St Pancras on 28 June 1975.

Class 66 No 66078 passes Kildale with the returning empty ballast train from the NYMR to Tees Yard on 8 March 2017. The house on the left and the spire of St Cuthbert's church are common to all three pictures.
John Spencer Gilks (2)/John Hunt

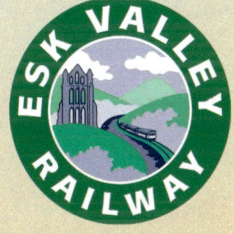

With Coate Moor as a backdrop, the 6.55am Whitby-Middlesbrough DMU drops down into Battersby on 4 May 1963, while at the same location on 1 December 2016 Class 156 No 156490 forms the 08.45 Whitby-Middlesbrough service. The railway cottage no longer has a warming fire as it has long since been demolished, and trees grow where the sidings used to be on the right. *John Boyes/John Hunt*

Grosmont to Battersby

Turning through 180 degrees, this is the view towards Battersby as a DMU accelerates away forming the 7.20am Middlesbrough-Scarborough service on 4 May 1963. On the left there used to be five sidings to accommodate the traffic generated by the Rosedale branch. Visible, too, is the three-road locomotive shed and water tower (the latter still standing in 2017).

As Class 156 No 156490 leaves forming the 10.27 Middlesbrough-Whitby service on 1 December 2016, the former sidings area and the Cleveland Hills are now largely obscured by tree growth, but the tree to the right of the DMUs is common to both pictures. *John Boyes/John Hunt*

Battersby to Picton

Battersby was once an important junction on the North Yorkshire & Cleveland Railway. The Picton to Stokesley section opened on 3 March 1857, but it was April 1858 before trains ran through to Battersby and on to Kildale. The line from Battersby to Picton was 12 miles in length and served intermediate stations at Ingleby, Stokesley, Sexhow, Potto, and Trenholm Bar. On 27 March 1861 a branch was opened from Battersby to serve the various mines in Rosedale West, and to Rosedale East in 1865, but when the mines were worked out the branch closed on 13 June 1929 and the rails were lifted. There was also a junction with the line from Middlesbrough, opened from Nunthorpe East Junction for goods traffic on 1 June 1864 and to passengers on 1 April 1868. A curve east of Battersby to allow through running, without the need for a reversal at the junction, was authorised in 1866 but never built.

The Picton line closed to passenger trains, suddenly, on 14 June 1954, though Trenholm Bar, Sexhow and Potto stations remained open for goods traffic until that, too, was discontinued, on 1 December 1958. However, wagons continued to be stored between Picton and Trenholm Bar and on the old up line between Ingleby and Stokesley. A goods service was maintained to Stokesley from the Battersby end until 2 August 1965, when it also ceased. After eventual removal of the stored wagons, the track was lifted throughout.

Looking north at Battersby in 1954 'A8' No 69858 (left) has arrived from Whitby, while on the right stands 'G5' No 67332, which has just run in on a Stockton-Whitby service via Picton. The junction between the Middlesbrough and Whitby lines is just beyond the signal box, and on the right, beyond the fence, are the remains of the Rosedale branch. *J. W. Armstrong*

Battersby to Picton

The first view of Battersby, looking south-west from the overbridge on the Middlesbrough line, is dated 4 May 1963, while the present-day picture is from 29 November 2016. The signals and the dominant locomotive shed are long gone, but the houses on either side of the coniferous trees to the right of the shed are still there. *John Boyes/John Hunt*

On the same day in 1954 as the pictures on page 100, 'G5' No 67332 has the road for Whitby with its train from Stockton via Picton, while 'A8' No 69858 is running round its Whitby-Middlesbrough train.

In the second picture 'T2' No 2238, hauling 'P3' No 2392 and 'K1' No 2005, takes water at Battersby in August 1975 en route from Grosmont to Shildon for the S&D 150 celebrations.

On 5 January 2017 Class 156 No 156451 arrives at Battersby forming the 08.45 Whitby-Middlesbrough service. Although the signals and signal box have gone, the water column is common to all three pictures. *J.W. Armstrong/John Hunt (2)*

On 21 April 1989 Class 143 No 143022 departs from Battersby as the 14.25 service from Whitby to Middlesbrough, while Class 47 No 47301 waits to depart to Grosmont.

In the second picture the '47' is hauling 'Deltic' No 55015 *Tulyar* and 'K1' No 2005, leaving behind No 37250, which had brought the consist from Thornaby. The diesels were en route to the NYMR's diesel gala that weekend. The signal box closed on 20 August 1989 when a colour-light signalling system was commissioned. Some of the semaphore signals were subsequently recovered by the NYMR. *Both David Warren*

The Gloucester DMU special of May 1976 waits in the evening sun to cross an incoming service train from Middlesbrough to Whitby.

In the second picture it is rush hour at Battersby on 7 April 1978 as interested onlookers – or passengers – watch the proceedings! On the right is No D5500, hauling a rather dead 'Q7' No 63460 en route from storage at Preston Park, Brighton, to the NYMR for restoration by the NELPG, waiting for the seemingly simultaneous arrival of trains from Whitby and Middlesbrough. *John Spencer Gilks/John Hunt*

Battersby to Picton

This is the west end of Battersby station in 1964, with the double track to Stokesley in the foreground, having just been used by the pick-up goods.

The same vantage point in 2014 shows the remnant of the Picton line as part of the present-day station's run-round loop. *John Boyes/John Hunt*

Looking towards Stokesley, the three-road engine shed still stands, there are wagons in the goods yard and passengers stand in anticipation of a passenger train on 4 May 1963.

Two years later, in the snow of 4 March 1965, the 6.55am service from Whitby to Middlesbrough has just arrived. The engine shed was demolished in December of that year, but while it had stood for 88 years it was only actually used to house locomotives for ten of them! *John Boyes/John Spencer Gilks*

Battersby to Picton

'B1' No 61031 *Reedbuck* has just run-round the SLS/RCTS 'North Eastern' rail tour on 2 May 1964, en route from Grosmont to Northallerton.

On 28 November 2016 'K1' No 62005, en route from Grosmont to Carnforth, stands at Battersby, having run round its support coach. *David Warren collection/John Hunt*

104 The North Yorkshire Moors and Esk Valley Railway Past and Present

No D6778 runs round the RCTS 'North Eastern No 3 Railtour' from Whitby before returning to Bradford on 6 May 1967. Note the tangerine NE Region colours on the destination boards.

On 28 February 2016 No D7628 performs the same manoeuvre while working an NYMR crew-training special from Grosmont. Trees now hide the Cleveland Hills and the traditional railway furniture has gone, except for the steam-age water column. *John Spencer Gilks/John Hunt*

At Ingleby on 14 June 1954 'G5' No 67288 propels its train out of one platform to continue its journey towards Stokesley on the near line, since the other was being used for wagon storage – so the porter is safe to jump down onto the track!
By 25 November 2016 the left-hand platform has disappeared. *J. W. Armstrong/John Hunt*

The same train, the 5.50pm Whitby-Stockton, stands at the platform before the setting-back manoeuvre seen in the previous picture.

Ingleby station building has been substantially altered, but the southern platform, complete with its waiting shelter, is still extant. *J. W. Armstrong/John Hunt*

Battersby to Picton

'G5' No 67240 stands in Stokesley station with a Whitby-Stockton train in May 1954. It is using the eastbound line as the westbound line at this time was being used for wagon storage.

On 25 November 2016 the station has a new lease of life and, as a result, is well preserved; behind the station building the goods shed also survives. *J.W. Armstrong/John Hunt*

We are now looking west at Stokesley station as 'G5' No 67343 enters with a Stockton to Whitby train in May 1954. The corresponding picture, taken on 25 November 2016, shows the refurbished building to good effect. *J.W. Armstrong/John Hunt*

The signal box, seen in the 'past' picture, has been preserved and relocated next to the house seen to the left of the signal. *John Hunt*

Battersby to Picton

109

Three miles west of Stokesley was Sexhow, seen here with 'A8' No 69858 on a Whitby-Stockton train in June 1954. Again the train is using the eastbound line, which because of wagon storage on the other line was effectively being worked as a single line between Ingleby and Picton.

On 25 November 2016, other than the road there is no visible evidence of the former railway. The station house, on the right, is extant and in private use. *J. W. Armstrong/John Hunt*

Potto was the next station towards Picton, and had staggered platforms on either side of a level crossing, as shown in the middle picture. In the first picture a group of passengers awaits the arrival of 'G5' No 67343 with a Stockton-Whitby train in the winter of 1953/54.

The third picture shows the well-preserved station buildings on 25 November 2016, now a private dwelling.
J.W. Armstrong (2)/John Hunt

Battersby to Picton

At Potto station, looking east in 1951, 'G5' No 67343 is heading a Whitby-Stockton service. Potto was the junction for the line to Whorlton mines, which branched off to the right; it closed in 1892, the rails being lifted in 1904.

In the same view on 25 November 2016, the former goods yard to the right is nowadays home to the well-known Preston's of Potto transport company. *J.W. Armstrong/John Hunt*

Between Potto and the next station at Trenholm Bar was Black Horse Crossing, seen here with 'B1' No 61034 *Chiru* on a Whitby-Stockton working on 14 June 1954, the final day of passenger working. Note the stored wagons on the former westbound track and the rotating signal, which showed red to road traffic when the gates were closed, and was identical to others on former NER lines, such as Low Marishes and Upper Carr south of Pickering.

The corresponding photograph shows the same view on 25 November 2016. *J. W. Armstrong/John Hunt*

Battersby to Picton

Looking west at Black Horse Crossing, 'G5' No 67333 heads east with a Stockton to Whitby service in the 1950s.

On 25 November 2016 the road and the crossing cottage remain as reminders of the railway's former presence, although the latter has been extended and modernised. *J.W. Armstrong/John Hunt*

Trenholm Bar station is seen first looking west on 21 November 1958, and the second picture shows 'J27' No 65861 working the eastbound pick-up goods through the station in June 1954.

Like Guisborough, it took some painstaking investigation to pinpoint the present-day viewpoints. Looking west on 29 November 2016 there is little to help identify the former station, except that the fence and remnants of a stone wall on the right are on the same alignment as the wall along the right-hand platform. *John F. Mallon/J.W. Armstrong/John Hunt*

'G5' 0-4-4T No 67345 leaves Trenholm Bar, wrong line, with the 5.50pm Whitby-Stockton train on 14 June 1954, while cars wait on the old A19 road.

Today the station house, almost unrecognisable, is on the right and the fence on the left marks the line of the old railway. The rest has been obliterated by the dualling of the A19 trunk road. *J.W. Armstrong/John Hunt*

116 The North Yorkshire Moors and Esk Valley Railway Past and Present

The line from Battersby joined the line from Northallerton at Picton. 'B1' No 61037 *Jairou* brings a Whitby-Stockton train off the Battersby line in the 1950s, while on 5 January 2017 Class 185 No 185128 heads north past the same spot as the 11.33 Manchester Airport-Middlesbrough service. *J. W. Armstrong/John Hunt*

In this view from the footplate of 'K1' No 62005 on 28 November 2016, the Battersby line used to diverge to the left and follow the fence to the left of the houses just visible to the left of the pylon. *John Hunt*

Battersby to Picton

Class 47 No 47833 heads south at Picton in January 1991. Seen from the same vantage point on 29 November 2016, a TransPennine Class 185 unit heads south as the 10.27 Middlesbrough-Manchester Airport service. As can be seen, The Station public house is still in business and the station house has been enlarged and renovated, both seen in the 'present' picture and from a different perspective from the footplate of 'K1' No 62005 on 4 April 2016. *John Spencer Gilks/John Hunt (2)*

Picton station building is seen first after the removal of the platforms in 1974, and again on 29 November 2016, showing that the road crossing is now automated and the station house has been considerably enlarged. *John Spencer Gilks/John Hunt*

Battersby to Picton

'G5' No 67343 surrenders the single-line token to the Picton signalman as it arrives with a train from Whitby in the 1950s. On 29 November 2016 Grand Central HST No 43428 heads north at the same spot as the 08.02 London King's Cross-Sunderland service. *J.W. Armstrong/John Hunt*

Northallerton-based 'D20' 4-4-0 No 62347 heads a pigeon van and passenger stock south past Picton signal box in the early 1950s, then on 5 January 2017 Class 185 No 185105 forms the 13.27 Middlesbrough-Manchester Airport service passing the same spot. *JWA Trust/John Hunt*

Battersby to Nunthorpe East Junction

Instigated by the North Yorkshire & Cleveland Railway, the 5½-mile Nunthorpe branch to Battersby was opened as a goods line by the NER in 1864 and for passenger services in 1868. The only intermediate station and crossing loop was at Great Ayton, and the line left the Middlesbrough-Guisborough line at Nunthorpe East Junction. Between there and Middlesbrough, a distance of another 5½ miles, there were two intermediate stations, at Nunthorpe itself and at Ormesby, but on 3 May 1976 a new halt was opened at Gypsy Lane, just three-quarters of a mile north of Nunthorpe. Ormesby was later renamed Marton, and on 18 May 2014 another new station was opened to serve the massive James Cook University hospital complex, situated between Marton and Middlesbrough.

North of Nunthorpe, in 2017 the Whitby service of four trains a day was augmented by local services to and from Newcastle, such that up to 17 trains traversed this section of line each way, every weekday.

Pictured from the long-demolished footbridge at Battersby, 'G5' No 67332 enters the station with an afternoon Stockton-Whitby train, via Picton, in 1954. The former branch to Rosedale ran between the station buildings and the wagons on the left and curved round to run in front of the terraced houses. *J.W. Armstrong*

On the curve leading into Battersby from the Middlesbrough direction during the harsh winter of 1963, a 'Q6'-hauled snow clearance train has stopped for workers to go about their business on 27 January.

At the same location, and in somewhat more benign weather conditions, a Metro-Cammell DMU forming the 7.20am Middlesbrough-Scarborough service approaches Battersby on 4 May 1963. *Both John Boyes*

Battersby to Nunthorpe East Junction

At the same location, Type 3 No D6899 brings 'Q6' No 63395 and ex-NCB No 29 into Battersby on 25 June 1970 en route from Thornaby to Grosmont and a new lease of life on the NYMR.

On 1 December 2016 Class 156 No 156490, forming the 10.28 Middlesbrough-Whitby service, rounds the curve into Battersby. *Both John Hunt*

With the line from Whitby in the background, Class 45 No 45121 leaves Battersby with a return excursion from Whitby to London St Pancras on 28 June 1975 ('K1' No 2005 had worked the train from Battersby to Whitby and back). In the bottom picture Class 66 No 66078, having run round its train in the station, returns empty ballast hoppers from the NYMR to Tees Yard on 8 March 2017. *John Spencer Gilks/John Hunt*

Battersby to Nunthorpe East Junction

In April 1983 Class 31 No 31240 passes the Battersby distant signal with the Tees Yard-Whitby pick-up goods, while in the present-day picture Class 66 No 66004 brings up the rear of empty ballast hoppers from the NYMR to Tees Yard headed by Class 66 No 66152 on 24 February 2017. *John Spencer Gilks/John Hunt*

126 The North Yorkshire Moors and Esk Valley Railway Past and Present

Great Ayton station is seen first looking south in 1963 – note the platform remains on the left and the distant Cleveland Hills.

In a similar view, No D6874 heads the Whitby-Tees Yard pick-up goods on 29 August 1972. Behind the diesel is 'P3' No 2392, which had hauled it and the train from Grosmont to Battersby and was destined for a Thornaby depot open day.

In the third view, two cyclists have alighted from Class 156 No 156451, which is working the 08.45 service from Whitby to Middlesbrough on 25 November 2016. Forty-four years after the middle picture, the station buildings have gone, and a simple shelter comprises the passenger facilities. *John Boyes/John Spencer Gilks/John Hunt*

Battersby to Nunthorpe East Junction

The outline of the Cleveland Hills is unmistakable in these two pictures taken 53 years apart. In the 1963 picture, the typical coal drops are in use and the station buildings extant.
 On 25 November 2016 the facilities are rather rudimentary but the remains of the coal drops can just be made out in the bushes beyond the fence. *John Boyes/John Hunt*

128 The North Yorkshire Moors and Esk Valley Railway Past and Present

At Nunthorpe East Junction, a mile east of Nunthorpe station itself, the Battersby line (on the left) joined the Middlesbrough to Guisborough line, seen here looking west on 27 April 1963. The 'present' picture from the same viewpoint is dated 1 December 2016; the line from Nunthorpe Junction to Guisborough (behind the camera) closed in 1964. *John Boyes/John Hunt*

Battersby to Nunthorpe East Junction

A Met-Cam DMU takes the Battersby line at Nunthorpe East Junction, also on 27 April 1963, forming the 7.20am Middlesbrough-Scarborough service; once onto the branch the track became single.

At the same location on 1 December 2016 Class 156 No 156490 forms the 10.28 Middlesbrough-Whitby service. *John Boyes/John Hunt*

In the 'past' picture, a DMU forming the 6.00pm Middlesbrough-Whitby services accelerates along the branch towards Great Ayton on 25 April 1963, as the signalman retrieves a roll of papers presumably thrown from the train. The corresponding present-day view was again taken on 1 December 2016. *John Boyes/John Hunt*

Nunthorpe to Guisborough

The Middlesbrough & Guisborough Railway was opened to passengers in 1854, originally with stations at Ormesby, Nunthorpe, Pinchinthorpe and Hutton Gate. Just beyond the latter, at Hutton Junction, half a mile from Guisborough, a line was opened to Boosbeck and Brotton, by the Cleveland Railway, in 1862. If through trains from Whitby and Loftus to Middlesbrough via the coast route called at Guisborough, they had to reverse at Hutton Junction, which involved propelling trains over the half-mile between the two.

The station at Pinchinthorpe closed completely on 29 October 1951, though like many of the well-built stations the main buildings survive in private residential use. No such fate would befall Guisborough; passenger trains were withdrawn on 2 March 1964, and goods services on 31 August the same year, by which time all goods traffic in the Boosbeck and Loftus area had also ceased. Subsequently, the whole Guisborough station site was completely cleared to make way for a new road, car parks and commercial development, leaving very little evidence – namely the low stone wall to Bow Street – of the former railway station's existence.

A view of Guisborough station on 16 February 1964. *John Spencer Gilks*

132 The North Yorkshire Moors and Esk Valley Railway Past and Present

This is Nunthorpe East Junction looking north-east towards Guisborough, and the 7.30am Guisborough-Middlesbrough DMU is approaching the junction on 27 April 1964.

On 1 December 2016 the similar view shows the single-track Battersby line in the foreground, while the trackbed of the former line to Guisborough is marked by the trees and bushes. *John Boyes/John Hunt*

Nunthorpe to Guisborough

Hutton Gate was one of two intermediate stations between Guisborough and Nunthorpe, the other being Pinchinthorpe. This is the view looking east on 12 February 1964, while the corresponding present view was taken on 5 January 2017. Note the substation common to both pictures. *John Spencer Gilks/John Hunt*

134 The North Yorkshire Moors and Esk Valley Railway Past and Present

On the same day these 'past' and 'present' pictures show the view looking west. The station house survives in private residential use, and the two platforms remain intact. *John Spencer Gilks/John Hunt*

Nunthorpe to Guisborough

The view westwards on 16 February 1964, taken from the bridge on the Guisborough line seen on the next page, shows Hutton Junction in the distance, with the line to Brotton and Loftus rising steeply to the left. After closure of Guisborough signal box in the 1930s, Hutton Junction was renamed Guisborough.

Following total closure on 31 August 1964 the area was redeveloped for housing and the bridge from which the picture was taken was demolished; the old railway line is now a public footpath. *John Spencer Gilks/ John Hunt*

This is the view westwards from the platform end at Guisborough on 16 February 1964, with the goods yard on the right.

On 25 November 2016 there is nothing to show that there was ever a railway here; the only recognisable feature is part of Guisborough Moor just visible to the left of the hipped-roof building in the 'present' picture. *John Spencer Gilks/John Hunt*

Nunthorpe to Guisborough

'A8' No 69886 enters Guisborough station with a Middlesbrough-Whitby train in August 1955.
   Only a low stone boundary wall onto Bow Street survives from the old station, which serves little purpose in helping to identify where the station stood in relation to the present layout. Today new roads, car parks and buildings have totally obliterated the old station site; again, only the distinctive outline of Guisborough Moor is common to both pictures. *J.W. Armstrong/John Hunt*

The same train as seen on the previous page reverses out of Guisborough in order to resume its journey to Loftus and the coastal route to Whitby; it will propel its train for the half-mile back to Hutton Junction.
Finding the equivalent vantage point in 2017 proved difficult. However, the ruin of Guisborough Priory, visible above the middle coach, can just be discerned through the trees above the white car in the car park. *J. W. Armstrong/John Hunt*

Nunthorpe to Guisborough

A DMU has just arrived at Guisborough station in 1963 with a service to Stockton; the passenger service was withdrawn on 2 March the following year.

The present-day view was taken on 25 November 2016. The terraced houses on the right and the single-storey building, partly in shadow, are common to both pictures. *John Spencer Gilks/John Hunt*

Nunthorpe to Middlesborough

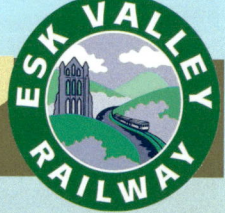

A special train comprising a Gloucester two-car DMU stands at Nunthorpe for photographs to be taken before resuming its journey to Whitby in May 1976.

In conjunction with the visit of a replica of Captain Cook's ship *Endeavour* to Whitby, a number of special trains were operated between Middlesbrough and Whitby on 12 December 1997 using preserved former Southern Region narrow-bodied 'Hastings' diesel-electric unit No 1001. It is pictured leaving Nunthorpe. *John Spencer Gilks/John Hunt*

Nunthorpe to Middlesborough

Contrasting weather conditions at Nunthorpe: in the first picture 'A4' No 60007 *Sir Nigel Gresley*, en route from Newcastle to Grosmont, waits for the late-running last train from Whitby, as the snow gets deeper and deeper, at 20.34 on 19 December 2009.

On an altogether more pleasant 18 February 2016, Class 156 No 156443 forms the 14.04 service from Middlesbrough to Whitby. *Both John Hunt*

With the iconic transporter bridge over the River Tees in the background, 'K1' No 62005 climbs away from Middlesbrough at North Ormesby with the 'Captain Cook Pullman' returning to Whitby in October 1999.

At the same spot on 4 January 2010 Class 66 No 66157 hauls a Kirow crane and, just visible, the new beams for the NYMR's bridge 30. *Both John Hunt*

Nunthorpe to Middlesborough

'Jubilee' No 5690 *Leander* revives memories of the Whitby pick-up goods as it heads a buffet car, wagons and a brake van away from Guisborough Junction, Middlesbrough, past the former Sadler & Co, Cleveland Chemical Works, bound for Grosmont and the NYMR, in July 1983.

In the comparison view, Class 142 No142065 forms the 10.30 Newcastle-Nunthorpe service on 29 November 2016. The line from Guisborough Junction to Nunthorpe was singled in 1986. *Both John Hunt*

144 The North Yorkshire Moors and Esk Valley Railway Past and Present

Middlesbrough station was opened on 3 October 1877 and incorporated a fine latticed-iron overall roof, with a grand lantern apex, regarded as a showpiece of architecture. However, it was badly bomb-damaged on 3 August 1942 and the surviving part was demolished in early 1954. The present rail side of the station dates from the rebuilding of 1960.

The driver of 'Q7' 0-8-0 No 63460 has a look round his engine in Middlesbrough station on 2 May 1964, prior to taking the RCTS 'North Eastern' tour to Newcastle via Wellfield. The 'Q7' had been specially reinstated for the day.

In the 'present' picture Class 185 No 185136 awaits departure as the 11.27 service to Manchester Airport on 29 November 2016. *David Warren collection/John Hunt*

Limited Edition

The NORTH YORKSHIRE MOORS RAILWAY people

The railways do not run without people, and the NYMR is no exception. In the succeeding pages some of the hundreds of people who have been engaged in running the railway since 1969 are depicted, at work in the various departments – motive power, carriage & wagon, permanent way, signals and telegraph, catering, and so on. There are also pictures showing the diverse range of activities associated with running the railway, such as special events, and some of the various awards and accolades that the railway has received over the years. Last but not least there are pictures of people at play since, after all, as many of those shown are volunteers, what they get out of it is satisfaction and enjoyment.

To set the scene, there are a couple of pictures of the old order – the men involved on the final day of revenue operation under the British Railways regime on 1 July 1966. It marked the end of an era – but soon a new one was to begin. As the NYMR celebrates its 50th anniversary, it continues to look to the future, and in that respect much depends on recruiting young blood to get involved in running the railway.

The future? Junior volunteers pose after a rewarding day working at the MPD on 21 August 2011. *Roger Swift*

The various crew members on the occasion of the final BR working on 1 July 1966 are seen here at Pickering. Diesel shunter No D2066 was en route from New Bridge Quarry back to Malton. Unfortunately, the photographer did not record the names. The building behind the '03' and brake van still stands today. *Both Frank Dean*

In all weathers: loading up a Hull & Barnsley Railway wagon at Grosmont on 7 December 1969, prior to being hauled up the line by *Salmon*, as shown in the second picture at Beckhole, with the other H&BR wagon and coach. *Nick Carter/David Birtle*

Relaying the turnout at the north end of Goathland station in March 1973 are Frank Carrington and Dick Morgan on the left, and on the right Paul Nelson, Graeme Reussner, Peter Brumby and Roy Lambeth. *Nick Carter*

At Goathland are John Hardy, Dave Birtle, Peter Robinson and Dick Oxlade, ready for a recovery run southwards on a railmotor in January 1970. *Nick Carter*

North Yorkshire Moors Railway People

Recovering track materials at Fen Bog in August 1972 are members of the Humberside Area Group together with John Nelson, Steve Todd and Paul Nelson on the right. *Nick Carter*

Two rail motors and trolleys carrying sleepers and rail at New Bridge on 12 November 1972, with Dick Morgan. *Nick Carter*

The inaugural run of AC Cars railbus No W79978 took place over the whole length of the line on 20 July 1969, only the third such movement since the line closed in 1965. In the first picture it is negotiating New Bridge level crossing, with John Randall taking the photo in the distance, together with Joe Brown and Tom Robertson on the crossing. In the second picture it has arrived at High Mill crossing at Pickering; pictured are Joe Brown, Paul Jamieson, Tom Salmon, Les Barwick, Tom Robertson, Nick Carter and Bill Clarke. *Both Nick Carter*

MPD staff Phil Naylor, Chris Kelly, Dougie Foster, Paul Whickham, Mark O'Brien, Chris Parrish and Charlie Dore pose next to No 76079's boiler on 26 June 2014.

Footplate training is an important role and doesn't just apply to NYMR staff. Here two Northern Ireland Railway drivers (kneeling) are being trained on steam on 19 May 2010. Standing are Chris Cubitt (NYMR and WCR), Johnny Glendenning (RPSI), Ron Smith (WCR Traction Inspector), Phil Crawshaw (NYMR) and Philip Benham (NYMR). *Both NYMR*

Clive Goult (left) and Dave Fawcett (right) present apprenticeship certificates to Paul Middleton and Adam Dalgleish at the MPD on 13 March 2014. *NYMR*

Chris Parrish does some machining in the MPD workshop on the same day. *John Hunt*

North Yorkshire Moors Railway People

Diesel fitter Dave Lee is at work on No D7628 on 31 January 2008. *John Hunt*

Members of the MPD pose next to recently outshopped No 45428 on 13 May 2010. *NYMR*

Young and not so young: fireman Matt Earnshaw and driver Noel Hartley on No 60103 *Flying Scotsman* on 16 March 2016, and driver Gerry Skelton on No 60019 *Bittern* on 10 May 2010. *Both John Hunt*

Carriage & wagon fitters Gordon Neale and John Watson work beneath a Mark 1 carriage at Pickering on 23 March 2009. *John Hunt*

Volunteer Dave Baxter restores a cattle wagon on 8 June 2013. *Ian Broadhead*

Kieran Murray works on a Mark 1 carriage bogie on 25 June 2013. *John Hunt*

Volunteer Mike Faulkner cuts rebates out of an oak tank wagon bolster, and Mark Toyne applies number transfers to an LNER teak coach. *Ian Broadhead/NYMR*

Track topics: in the first picture the PW team is in the throes of relaying track at Beckhole on 24 January 2008, while on 12 June 2011 members of the Levisham Station Group Wombles are Kevin Wood, Geoff North, Stephen Mason, Simon Waddington, Michael Thompson and Brian Woodburn jacking and packing the north siding at Levisham. *John Hunt/Simon Barraclough*

Modern tools of the trade: the ballast regulator, operated by Nick Carter, is at work north of Levisham on 20 March 2012, and the tamper at Levisham on 22 February 2012. *Bryan Blundell/NYMR*

The night shift: it is difficult, if not impossible, especially when trains are running, to have possession of the track to carry out major works, so night working is resorted to. In the first picture the tamper is at work in a blizzard – far from ideal conditions, but very necessary.

In the second picture Stephen Mason and Simon Barraclough are lifting old sleepers out of the level crossing at Levisham on 2 February 2012 as part of the renewal of the rails, sleepers and ballast before the rubber crossing panels were installed. *NYMR/Simon Barraclough*

Signals & telegraph: no trains can move without the authority of the signaller, so the S&T department has a crucial role to play. In the first picture, Alex Pickering, John Freear, Richard Owen, Jim Beaumont and Ray Halmshaw are putting the fittings on the new signal 'dolls' (short posts) for the former Scarborough Falsgrave gantry, re-sited at Grosmont.

In the second view Ray Halmshaw, Jim Beaumont, Richard Owen, Paul Gammon, John Freear and Malcolm Kitchin pose by the gantry after fitting the signal motors. *Both Craig Donald*

Within sight of the signal box, S&T engineers Jim Beaumont, Paul Gammon and Malcolm Kitchin are replacing one of the level crossing gates at Grosmont on 14 June 2012. *Craig Donald*

In rather more inclement weather conditions, the S&T team of Paul Gammon, Ray Halmshaw, Jim Beaumont, Malcolm Kitchin and Craig Donald take a break from drilling new rails for track circuit wires near New Bridge on 14 February 2013. *Craig Donald*

Station Group volunteers prepare the concrete foundations for the new shop at Goathland on 19 July 2016. *John Hunt*

Following the successful replacement of bridge 30, between Grosmont and Goathland, the new structure was officially 'opened' on 19 April 2010, the ceremony being performed by Pete Waterman, on the right. *John Hunt*

North Yorkshire Moors Railway People

The Duke of Gloucester unveils the plaque to mark the completion of the reinstatement of the G.T. Andrews-style overall roof at Pickering station on 4 October 2011, while in the second view the ribbon is cut to mark the opening of the learning and visitor centre on Platform 2 at Pickering on 22 October 2010. *Both John Hunt*

The formal opening of the new second platform at Whitby occurred on 6 March 2015, to coincide with the celebrations to mark the 50th anniversary of the closure of the Pickering line on 8 March 1965. Cutting the ribbon is BBC *Look North* presenter Harry Gration. *John Hunt*

On 26 November 2009 the NYMR received the Visitor Attraction of the Year award at the Yorkshire Moors & Coast Tourism Partnership Awards ceremony. *NYMR*

North Yorkshire Moors Railway People

The Railway's S&T department won the prestigious Siemens Signalling Award, presented during the National Railway Heritage Awards ceremony held in Merchant Taylor's Hall, London, on 2 December 2015. Here the S&T team, headed by Dave Torbet (holding the plaque), pose for the official camera. *NYMR*

Suitably attired to celebrate the 175th anniversary of the opening of the Whitby & Pickering Railway on 26 May 2011 are Lesley and Philip Benham, Bryan Draper, Jim Dedicoat and Mary Clarke. *NYMR*

TV personalities: Michael Palin takes centre stage with driver Dave Ratcliffe, fireman John Hunt and the owner of No 4767, Ian Storey on 1 June 1980. In the second photograph Michael Portillo is seen being filmed in conversation with driver Chris Cubitt on 9 June 2010. *Both NYMR*

North Yorkshire Moors Railway People

BBC *Look North* presenter Harry Gration and former work colleague Alan Whitehouse share a joke at Pickering on 6 March 2015. *John Hunt*

Outgoing General Manager Philip Benham (left) shakes hands with his successor, Chris Price, on 30 September 2015. *John Hunt*

Rudolph and Santa try to outrun a Santa Special at Grosmont on 20 December 2014, while steam from No 45212 is used to clear points of snow at Grosmont on 20 December 2009. *John Colls/John Hunt*

North Yorkshire Moors Railway People

Members of the Grosmont Station Group pose on 24 August 2014, featuring Tom Sayers, Alan Sanderson, Steve Dymott, Mike Franks, Peter Robinson, Brian Metherell, Victor Wood, John Alexander (rear), Ronnie Metherell, Trish Franks (seated), and Brian Carter. *Tom Sayers*

A meeting of the NYMR branch of the RMT union in the Crossing Club at Grosmont on 23 February 2009. *NYMR*

Special events: a Mad Hatter's tea party at Grosmont in front of 'J72' No 69023, and the NAAFI on Platform 2 at Pickering during Wartime Weekend on 16 October 2010. *Both NYMR*

North Yorkshire Moors Railway People

Cow Wath bridge at Goathland undergoes a 'load test' as No 60103 *Flying Scotsman* departs on 13 March 2016. *Maurice Burns*

The Tour de Yorkshire at Grosmont, 1 May 2016. *John Hunt*

Long service: the NYMR acknowledges the long service of its volunteer and paid staff. John Meredith, long-serving volunteer and former editor of *Moors Line*, the Trust's house magazine, celebrates on 3 May 2016 with his wife Pat, who was 80 that day.

In the second picture, volunteers proudly hold their long-service certificates in front of No 63395 at Pickering on 25 October 2015. *John Hunt/Mike Braham*

Catering: the Goathland station beer tent in full swing, with Station Master John Bruce and Margaret Braham pulling the pints. The second picture depicts service aboard the railway's prestige Pullman dining train on 26 June 2009. *Mike Braham/NYMR*

Catering: Margaret Braham serves a Japanese TV crew in the Warehouse tea room at Goathland station, and Linda, Jan and Julie are ready to serve refreshments to Santa Special passengers at Pickering on 19 December 2010. *Mike Braham/Andrew Frith*

Paul Hughes makes a purchase from Lucy Robertson, who is manning a sales stall on 11 October 2014 to raise funds for the restoration of No 3672 *Dame Vera Lynn*. *John Robertson*

Operations Manager Norman Hugill presents a certificate to signaller David Birchall in New Bridge signal box on 28 June 2008. *NYMR*

The future: Junior Volunteers are the future lifeblood of the NYMR. In the first picture a group of JVs has been rebuilding stone boundary walls near Goathland on 29 July 2016.

Earlier in the year, on 9 April, NELPG Junior Volunteers Ethan Humble, Noah Hunter, Dylan Bonnet, Tom Houseman, Rob Sowden, Henry Pritchard and Tom Noble pose in front of the 'Q6' after cleaning it at Grosmont. *Sam Kendall/Tom Noble*

List of Subscribers

A

Richard Alcock
David A. Alexander
John Alexander
Ian Allan Bookshop (Birmingham)
John M. Allen
Charles Allenby
Malcolm Allison
Ian James Allison
Mr Keith Archer
Mark Arscott
Norman Ashfield
A. R. Askew
David Aspinall
Paul Astell
Alan Ashwood
Philip Atkinson
Colin Atkinson
Keith R. Attwood
Michael Auton

B

Anders Rytter Bach
Ian Baggott
M. J. Bailey
Laird of Bandrum NTSR Station Master
Colin Barker
Mr and Mrs L. J. Barnes
Mike Barnes
David and Sylvia Barthorpe
Richard Barron
Peter Barsby
Robert Batchelor
David Bate
Stephen R. Batty
Patrick Bedwell
Chris Beicher
David C. Bent
Peter Birdsall
Bertram Books Ltd
Ian Blair
Simon Blanchard

List of Subscribers

Bert Blower
Stephen Bonnington
A. J. Booker
David Boot
Bryan Booth
Andrew J. M. Boulton
Peter and Clare Bowes
Craig Bownes
Jonathan Bradley
Andrew Braid
Paul Brereton
Terence Breton
Dennis Brewer
M. Brown
Stuart David Brown
Mr C. and Mrs B. Brummitt
Vincent Bulmer
J. A. Burdon-Cooper
Bob Burgess
Phillip and Lucille Burness
Chris Burrow
David J. Buttle
John Byrne

C

Stephen Calvert
Stephen Calvert
Mr Andrew Carpenter
John Carr
Nick Carter
Ken and Jane Catchpole
Andrew Cattell
G. H. Catterick
Sue and Graeme Cook
Jim Cook
Alan Corben
David Corfield
Ben Couldwell
Jon Cousens
Mr Robert Crisp
J. Graham Crosby
Clive G. Cross
Phillip Crossland
Stephen Croucher
John Cudlipp
Tom and Peta Cunningham

List of Subscribers

D

Colin Davenport
Michael Dawesg
Peter Dealtry
Michael J. Denholm
Geof Dickson
Les Dobson
J. C. Doubleday
Raymond Dover
Len Dowson
Brian Dowthwaite
Dr. Mike Draisey

E

Joseph William Easterby
David Edmondson
David Elliott
David Emmerson
Esk Valley Railway Development Company

F

James Ferrabee
Mike Fish
Charles F. Fisher
Mr Robert and Mrs Susan Fitzsimmons
J. C. Fleming
John Freear

G

Paul and Valerie Gardner
Gardners Books Ltd
Chris Gee
Derek Gilbert
Trevor Goodall
Robert S. Goulding
Alan B. Graham
Dave J. Gray
Chris Grayson
M. A. Green
Grosmont Bookshop
Basil Groundsell

List of Subscribers

H

Michael and Gloria Hair
Ray and Jennifer Halmshaw
Philip and Margaret Hamerton
M. Hancock
John Hanson
Happy Retirement Ian xx
Dad/Grandad Harding
Philip Hardwick
Colin Harness
Anthony Hart
R.W. Haslett
Peter Hawkins
Andrew Hazel
Geoff Hemingway
Mike Heath
Jim Henderson
Peter HIll
David Hilton
Michael Hobbs
Leslie John Holstead
David Holt
Gordon Homer
Nigel Hopwood

Frank Horsfield
Donald Horsfield
Phil Horton
Clive Howard
Reverend Miles Howarth
Steve Hubin
Geoff Hughes
Stephen Hughes
Stephen Hone
Michael "Owl" Hurst
Dave Hutchinson

I

Richard Irons

J

Tony Jackson
Paul Jameson
Ray Johnson
Robin Johnson
Lawrence Jones
James Jones

List of Subscribers

K

Michael Kain
David Karfoot
Nelson Keen
Ron Kenyon
Malcom and Karin Kilpatrick
Graham King
Douglas John Kipling
Colin J. Kirby
Mark Kirby

L

Warren Lake
Peter Lane
John and Christine Lardner
Chris Lawson
Roger Lazenby
Richard Leckie
Christopher Lindley
Phil Littler
Mike Lloyd
Michael J. Lloyd
Martin Lloyd
Raymond Lonergan
Chris Lorek
C. G. M. Lougee

M

Julian Maddogs-Born
Stephen Maltby
David Mark
Richard W. Marsden
Kevin McCauley
MDS Book Sales
William Middleton
George Adrian Mitchell
Richard Moore
Tony Muxlow

N

George Nelles Ex NYMR Guard
Robert Noakes
Malcolm Noble

List of Subscribers

O

Mark Ogden
John Oliver
Maureen and Brian Ovington
Michael Oxley

P

Bob and Chris Patterson
Dr R. Pearce
Phil and Jackie Pease
Mr P. Phillips
Peter J Phillips
Robert Pitt
Jack Popplewell

R

Elizabeth Ragsdale 1937-2009
Norman Raine
Stephen Rhodes
Mr D. J. Rice
Mark Richards
Bella Richardson
Mark Richardson
Jonathan Roberts
Peter William Robinson
Ieuan Roden
Anthony Rosier
Michael Rowley
Keith Russell
Don Ryder

S

Mike Sanders
Michael Sanderson
Clive Scorer
Lolnruss Scott

Paul Scrimshaw
Nigel and Alex Seary
Mark Senior
Geoffrey Selwyn
Andrew Sewell
Peter Sharman
Pam and Stuart Shepherd
Hilary Sherlock
Mr Chris Shilliam
Phillip Short
Anthony Silson
Mark Sissons
Alastair Smith
Andrew Smith
Richard L. Smith
James Smith
Rob Sowden
John Spalding
Alan Speight
Peter G. Spence
Tom Stanforth
RAV Staples
Mike Steele
Peter Stoddart
John Stokes
Frederick Storr
Jens Strain
David Stringer
Colin Sturman
Mike Swinnerton

T

Stuart Talton
Richard Taylor
John Taylor
Karl Thompson
Richard John Thompson
R. G. Thornton
Robert Thould

The North Yorkshire Moors Railway and The Esk Valley Line Past and Present

List of Subscribers

David Burchett and Christine Tiffany
Richard Turton
Steve Tysoe

U

Eric Edward Upton

V

Ian Varty

W

Antony Wakeford
David Wallace
Robert Walsh
Peter Walton
John H. Ward
Kevin Ward
Stephen John Ward
Robert Ward
Daniel Waterman
Waterstones Booksellers
Chris Watkinson
Angela Watson

Dr Graeme Watson
Jim Waugh
Helen Webb
Keith Webster
P. F. Welburn
Richard Wheeler
M. W. Whitaker
Graham S. Whitaker
Mark White
Stephen R. Wilkins
Dora Wilkinson
Martyn Wilkinson
Mr A. Willison
Chris Wilson
John F. Wilson
J. Christopher Wilson
Andy and Kerrie Wood
Victor Wood
Paul Wood
Vince Wright

Y

Rob Yarnall
Derek J. A. Young

Captions for pages i-v

Author signature page
'A8' No 69866 has just taken water from the water column, which is still extant in 2017, at Battersby with an evening train for either Middlesbrough or Whitby. Note the long since removed bay platform line with engine release on the right. *J. W. Armstrong*

Page i
A 156 unit near Houlsyke forming the 10.28 service from Middlesbrough to Whitby on 23 January 2017. *John Hunt*

Page ii
LMS 5XP No 5690 *Leander* attracts admiring onlookers of all ages as it prepares to run round its train at Battersby in July 1983; it was en route to the NYMR at Grosmont. *John Hunt*

Page iii
'K4' No 61994 *The Great Marquess* leads 'B1' No 61264 near Danby with a special train from York to Whitby on 22 March 2014. *John Hunt*

Page iv
LMS 5MT No 44871 at Kildale Moor on the climb from Commondale with a special NYMR dining train from Grosmont to Battersby and back on 22 March 2015. *John Hunt*

Page v
'Q6' No 63395 and NCB No 29, hauled by a Class 37, drop down towards Lealholm on 20 June 1970, en route to a new lease of life on the NYMR. *John Hunt*

Index of locations and locomotive classes

LOCATIONS

Battersby 5, 6, 16, 66, 67, 69, 71, 72, 73, 75, 77, 78, 79, 81, 83, 85, 86, 87, 88, 89, 91, 93, 94, 95, 96, 97, 98, 99, 100, 101, 103, 105, 107, 109, 111, 113, 115, 116, 117, 119, 121, 122, 123, 124, 125, 126, 127, 128, 129, 132
Beckhole 8, 27, 147, 157
Birmingham 90
Black Horse Crossing 112, 113
Bog Hall 7, 8, 12
Borrows well tank 24
Bradford 85, 104

Castleton 6, 66, 80, 83, 84, 85, 86
Castleton Moor 66
Commondale 66, 86, 88, 89, 90

Danby 66
Darnholm 29
Derby 5
Deviation signal box 26

East Rosedale 66
Egton 67

Farwath 49
Fen Bog 2, 38, 39, 149
Forge Valley line 8

Glaisdale 20, 66, 68, 69, 70, 71, 72, 73, 74, 80
Goathland 4, 5, 8, 19, 21, 23, 25, 27, 29, 30, 31, 32, 33, 34, 35, 36, 37, 39, 43, 47, 49, 51, 83, 148, 162, 171, 173, 174, 176
Grand Central HST 119
Great Ayton 121, 126, 130
Grosmont 5, 6, 8, 9, 11, 13, 15, 17, 19, 20, 21, 22, 23, 24, 25, 26, 27, 29, 30, 31, 32, 33, 35, 36, 38, 40, 46, 49, 51, 53, 56, 63, 66, 67, 69, 71, 73, 75, 77, 78, 79, 80, 81, 83, 85, 87, 88, 89, 90, 91, 93, 95, 98, 99, 103, 104, 123, 126, 141, 143, 147, 160, 161, 162, 168, 169, 170, 171, 176
Guisborough 5, 6, 89, 90, 114, 121, 128, 131, 132, 133, 135, 136, 137, 138, 139, 143

Helmsley 8
Hungate 58, 59
Hutton Gate 131, 133
Hutton Junction 138
Ingleby 66, 96, 105, 106, 109

Kildale 66, 87, 88, 89, 90, 91, 93, 96
Kildale Moor 66, 87, 88

Larpool 14
Lealholm 66, 74, 75, 76, 77, 78, 79
Leeds 5, 6, 28, 31, 49, 66
Levisham 8, 19, 20, 34, 36, 42, 44, 45, 46, 47, 48, 50, 157, 158, 159
Lingdale 66
Loftus 6, 8, 131, 135, 138
London King's Cross 8, 8, 42, 42, 119, 119
Lyke Wake Walk 2, 38

Malton 2, 5, 6, 8, 11, 25, 30, 33, 38, 42, 47, 52, 55, 57, 59, 60, 61, 63, 64, 65, 146
Marishes Road 60, 61, 62
Middlesbrough 2, 5, 6, 8, 12, 13, 15, 17, 67, 72, 74, 75, 76, 80, 81, 82, 83, 84, 85, 86, 89, 90, 91, 93, 94, 95, 96, 97, 98, 99, 100, 102, 116, 117, 120, 121, 122, 123, 126, 128, 129, 130, 131, 132, 137, 140, 141, 142, 143, 144
Mill Lane 8
Mirvale 8, 23, 24, 25
Moorgates 36

New Bridge 5, 36, 37, 39, 43, 47, 49, 50, 51, 56, 58, 146, 149, 150, 161, 175
Newcastle 13, 87, 121, 141, 143, 144
Northdale 38
Nunthorpe 5, 6, 66, 96, 121, 123, 125, 127, 128, 129, 131, 132, 133, 135, 137, 139, 140, 141, 143
Nunthorpe East Junction 96, 121, 123, 125, 127, 128, 129, 132

Pickering 5, 6, 8, 9, 11, 14, 15, 18, 21, 23, 25, 28, 30, 32, 33, 35, 36, 37, 39, 40, 43, 47, 49, 50, 51, 52, 54, 55, 56, 57, 58, 59, 60, 61, 63, 65, 66, 112, 146, 150, 155, 160, 163, 164, 165, 167, 170, 172, 174
Pickering High Mill 40
Picton 2, 5, 6, 66, 86, 96, 97, 98, 99, 101, 103, 105, 107, 109, 110, 111, 113, 115, 116, 117, 118, 119, 120, 121
Pilmoor 8
Potto 96, 110, 111, 112
Preston Park, Brighton 100
Preston's of Potto 111

Rillington 6, 8, 60, 63
Rillington Junction 6, 8, 63
River Esk 7, 14, 15, 16, 17, 66, 68, 73, 74, 80
Rosedale 66, 95, 96, 121
Ruswarp 8, 17

Scarborough 6, 8, 13, 63, 64, 65, 95, 122, 129, 160
Seamer 8
Settle & Carlisle line 22
Skinningrove 85
Sleights 18
Stockton 68, 96, 98, 106, 107, 108, 109, 110, 111, 112, 113, 115, 116, 121, 139
Stokesley 66, 96, 101, 102, 105, 107, 108, 109

Tees Yard 20, 34, 78, 80, 90, 93, 124, 125, 126
The Grange 44
Thornaby 70, 78, 99, 123, 126
Trenholm Bar 96, 112, 114, 115
Tweedmouth MPD 26
Tyseley 90

Water Ark 28
West Rosedale 66, 66

Whitby 2, 5, 6, 7, 8, 9, 10, 11, 12, 13, 14, 15, 16, 17, 18, 21, 22, 26, 28, 31, 38, 42, 46, 49, 54, 60, 63, 66, 67, 68, 69, 70, 71, 72, 73, 74, 75, 76, 77, 78, 80, 81, 82, 83, 84, 85, 86, 87, 88, 89, 90, 91, 93, 94, 95, 96, 98, 99, 100, 102, 104, 106, 107, 108, 109, 110, 111, 112, 113, 115, 116, 119, 121, 123, 124, 125, 126, 129, 130, 131, 137, 138, 140, 141, 142, 143, 164, 165
York 7, 8, 22, 25, 38, 46, 54, 63, 65, 70, 90

LOCOMOTIVE CLASSES

4MT 65 **Barclay 0-6-0** 24
5MT 9, 52, 54
BR Standard 2-6-0 12
BR Standard 2-6-4T 56
'Castle' Class 55 **Class 'A3'** 27
Class 'A4' 21, 141
Class 'A8' 4-6-2T 91
Class 'B1' 7, 9, 11, 13, 25, 28, 37, 38, 42, 53, 54, 71, 79, 87, 88, 103, 112, 116
Class 'Deltic' 13, 99
Class 'D20' 4-4-0 120
Class 'D49' 47
87, 88, 123
Class 'G5' 68, 71, 96, 98, 105, 107, 108, 110, 111, 113, 115, 119, 121
Class 'J52' 28, 35, 90
Class J72' 40, 40, 170, 170
Class 'K4' 6, 15, 49, 87, 88
Class 'P3' 19, 23, 24, 52, 56, 70, 78, 84, 87, 90, 98, 126
Class 'Q6' 21, 24, 32, 37, 42, 49, 79, 87, 88, 122, 123, 176
Class 'Q7' 0-8-0 144
Class 'T2' 42, 98
Class 'V2' 52, 53
Class 14 40
Class 24 31, 84, 90
Class 31 22, 89, 90, 125
Class 37 79, 85, 88, 90
Class 40 63
Class 45 124
Class 47 20, 83, 99, 117
Class 66 10, 20, 34, 67, 70, 80, 83, 93, 124, 125, 142
Class 142 17, 143
Class 143 21, 99
Class 144 80
Class 156 72, 74, 75, 76, 80, 81, 82, 83, 84, 85, 86, 89, 90, 91, 94, 95, 98, 123, 126, 129, 141
Class 185 64, 116, 117, 120, 144
Class 220 35
ex-NCB 19, 23, 24, 32, 45, 53, 56, 79
'Hall' Class 63
'Hastings' DMU 89, 140
HST 5, 119
Hudswell Clark 0-4-0 24
'Jubilee' Class 85, 143
LMS 2-6-4T 22
LNER 'Pacific' 29
'Pacer' 82
'Schools' Class 70, 73, 77